The Great

Mughal Emperors

Compiled by Mrs Rungeen Singh

YLP

Young Learner Publications™

G-1 Rattan Jyoti,
18 Rajendra Place,
New Delhi -110008 (INDIA)
Ph.: 25750801, 25820556
Fax: 91-11-25764396

Printed at : Kumar Offset Printers, Delhi-110092

CONTENTS

THE GOLDEN BIRD

In the olden days, India was known as 'sone ki chiriya' or the golden bird because of the immense richness of its natural resources.

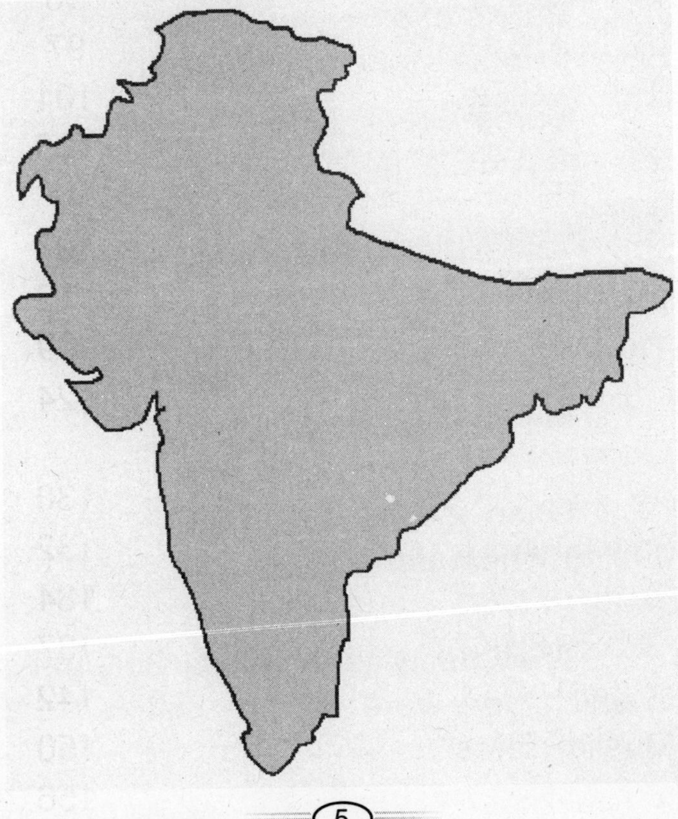

Towards the north of India lies the high and long Himalayan mountain range.

These mountains prevented people from entering India but the Khyber Pass and the Bolan Pass in the mountains made it possible for many people to invade India.

Rulers of other countries wanted to come to India to plunder its wealth.

Some Greek rulers like Alexander the Great in 326 B.C. came just for a short time.

Other invaders to arrive in ancient India were Scythians, Kushans and Huns. They established few kingdoms in India.

Mahmud of Ghazni and Mohammad Ghori also came to loot India.

Ghori left behind some governors due to which the Muslim rule started in India.

They ruled as the Delhi Sultunate, in which there were many dynasties of the Muslim rulers.

Then came the Mughals in 1526 under Babur, and they ruled in India for a long time.

The Mughals came from what is now known as Uzbekistan. They changed the history of India.

Then from the sea route came the Portuguese, the French and the British.

The Mughal Emperor Jahangir allowed the British to trade in India when Sir Thomas Roe asked him for permission.

This gave way to the British rule in India after the first Battle of Plassey in 1757. The British conquered nearly the whole of India.

Till the year 1857 the Mughals continued to rule. The Britishers then removed the last Mughal Emperor and sent him to Rangoon.

The British ruled India till 15th August, 1947 when India got its independence.

BABUR AND GURU NANAK

It is said that the great Guru Nanak met Babur.

When he met Guru Nanak, Babur had not yet become the Emperor of India.

Babur was a king of what is now called Uzbekistan.

He had come to invade the city of Saidpur (now known as Eminabad) in 1521.

Guru Nanak, the first Sikh guru, was then on his travels to spread his teachings to countries beyond India.

When Guru Nanak came to Saidpur to meet his follower Lalo, he saw mutilated bodies lying around, women crying and houses destroyed. All these were the consequences of Babur's military attack.

Seeing the widespread destruction caused by Babur, Guru Nanak was pained. He condemned this barbarous act in strong words.

Guru Nanak and Mardana were caught by Babur's soldiers and taken into prison. There they saw many old people suffering.

Despite being sick and tired, the old people had to work hard in the prison. In the prison, Guru Nanak was asked to grind grain using grinding stones. Guru Nanak sat down and started singing hymns.

After sometime people saw that the grinding stones were moving on their own.

Everyone present in the prison room bowed their heads, knowing that they were witnessing a great miracle.

Some people say that when this news was given to Babur, he asked Guru Nanak to meet him.

Others say that Babur heard Guru Nanak sing a sad song, and this had an effect on him. He said, "Bring this man here. His song touches my heart."

When Guru Nanak was brought to him, Babur asked what he had been singing about.

Guru Nanak told him that he had sung to God about the sufferings of the prisoners.

When Babur asked him if he wanted something to eat, Guru Nanak replied that his hunger was satisfied only by God.

Whatever be true, the fact is that the great Sikh guru, Guru Nanak, met the Mughal Emperor, Babur.

Guru Nanak told Babur that there was no point in being a king and conquering other kingdoms.

He said that kings should not be proud or cruel. They should take the path of righteousness and be kind to their people.

On hearing Guru Nanak, Babur realised that he had treated the prisoners badly. He asked Guru Nanak, “I have done wrong. What should I do now?”

Guru Nanak said, “Let the prisoners go and give their lands back to them.”

Babur did what Guru Nanak told him to do. He freed all the prisoners he had imprisoned while invading their cities.

Then he asked Guru Nanak, “You are a holy man. Tell me, will I ever become the Emperor of India?”

Nanak replied, “Yes, you will become the Emperor of India. But you must treat the people well.”

Babur respected the Sikh guru a lot, so he promised to be a just and kind ruler. Babur instructed his soldiers to free Guru Nanak and Mardana.

BABUR AND IBRAHIM LODI

Babur had attacked the border areas of India four times before he finally came to India in 1526 A.D.

At that time Muslim rulers were ruling in the Northern part of India.

The Qutub Minar had already been made in Delhi by the first Delhi Sultan Qutub-ud-din Aibak.

The rulers from the Slave dynasty to the Lodi dynasty are called the Delhi Sultunate.

Ibrahim Lodi, the son of Sikandar Lodi, was the last king of the Lodi dynasty to rule in North India.

There was a group of nobles who were against Ibrahim Lodi. He inspired a feeling of anger in the nobility by replacing old commanders with new ones who were loyal to him.

Ibrahim Lodi did not inherit the ruling capabilities of his father, Sikandar Lodi. He was not strong enough to manage the people who rebelled against him.

His nobles asked Babur to invade India and help them dethrone Ibrahim Lodi.

Babur agreed to invade India and dethrone Ibrahim Lodi on their invitation, as he had always dreamt of conquering India.

So for the fifth time Babur came to invade India.

Babur fought Ibrahim Lodi on the field of Panipat (now in Haryana) on 21st April, 1526. It is called the first Battle of Panipat, and it initiated the Mughal rule in India.

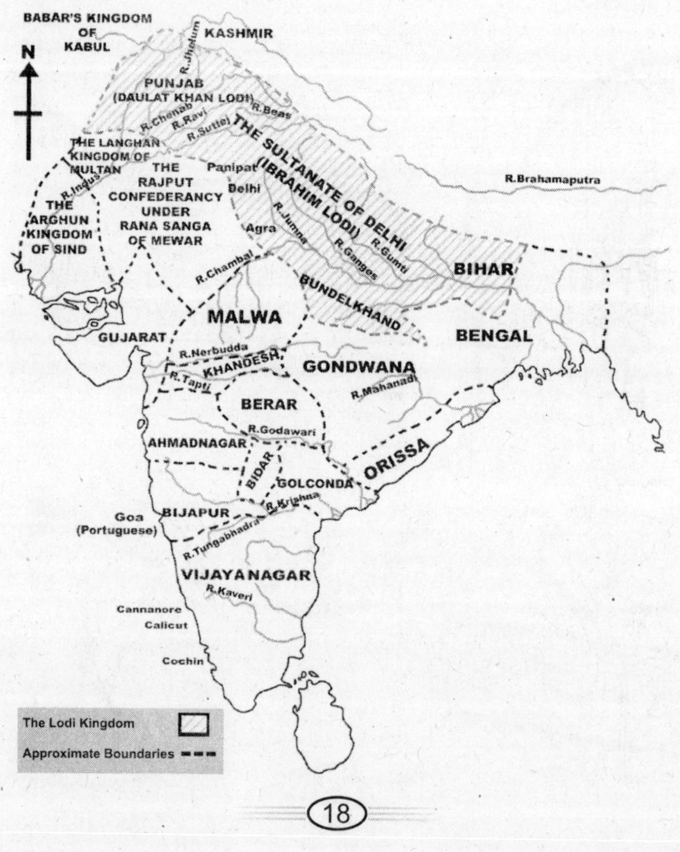

Ibrahim Lodi had a big army of 100,000 soldiers and 1500 elephants. He made his army stand together in a rectangle, as he was not very efficient in planning.

On the other hand, Babur was not only a clever warrior but also a good army leader.

Humayun told Babur, "We are lesser in number than them."

Babur replied, "We might be lesser in number, but we are superior in skill."

Babur had only some artillery and 12,000 soldiers. Out of them the cavalry army on horses was divided into three groups.

One group of soldiers had to ride along the sides and attack the Lodi army from the back. The other two groups had to attack the Lodi army from the sides.

Babur used his small army very efficiently. He placed big guns called cannons in a line in front of his army when it faced the Lodi army.

In India, people were not used to such weapons.

Lodi did not know how to fight this attack from all sides. His army was badly hit by the quick and efficient Mughals.

As Babur attacked, many of Lodi's soldiers were killed. The remaining ran away, after being chased by Babur's fast horsemen. A general of Ibrahim's army came to Ibrahim and said, "Your Majesty, your life is precious. If we lose, you can always form another army later and fight."

But Ibrahim Lodi said, "No, I cannot go away. See, there are so many people fighting for me, I cannot leave them." So he fought on.

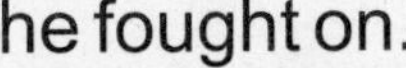

When Babur was informed about Ibrahim Lodi's death during the battle, he said to his soldiers, "Take me to his dead body."

On seeing Ibrahim Lodi lying dead on the ground, Babur bent down and lifted his head with his hands and said, "He was a brave king. I will give him the funeral befitting a king. I will also make a tomb for him."

Thus ended the rule of Ibrahim Lodi, the last ruler of the Delhi Sultunate.

Babur became the first Mughal Emperor to rule over a part of North India around Delhi and Agra.

After his victory in the Battle of Panipat, Babur ruled only for four years. He did not spend much time in India. He was a brave and kind ruler.

His body was very fit and strong. He is said to have swum nearly every big river in India and that too often against the current.

He was so healthy and fit that he could carry two people, one on each shoulder, and run or even climb a slope.

BABUR AND RANA SANGA

Babur successfully invaded Delhi and Agra. After this entry into North India, Babur had to face the Indian kings who stood up against him as he was an invader coming from a foreign land.

The Rajputs were brave and loved their freedom and honour. Rana Sanga of Mewar united various Rajput states to fight against Babur. He did this as he did not want the Mughals in India.

Rana Sanga is known in history not only for being a great warrior, but also for his chivalric and generous nature.

His chivalric nature is well reflected in the fact that he gave back the kingdom of Sultan Mahmud of Mandu after defeating him and taking him as a prisoner.

Rana Sanga had lost an eye and an arm during a battle. He also had many scars of wounds on his body which were proofs of his bravery. But despite all his injuries he fought with great courage.

Babur had to fight Rana Sanga, whose army consisted of 210,000 soldiers. He knew that it would not be easy to win against Rana Sanga.

Babur felt that he could win only if he could instil the feeling of courage in the minds of his soldiers. So he declared that he would not touch wine till he won the battle. He had all the wine drained away.

The soldiers felt that when their king was doing so much, they should also fight the battle with all their might.

They all fought very bravely against the Rajputs at the Battle of Khanua, near Agra.

Rana Sanga lost to Babur in the Battle of Khanua on 10th March, 1527.

After that Babur won over Mahmud Lodi at the Battle of Ghagra River on 6th May, 1529.

Thus, he won a large kingdom in North India. He was a good king, but he repeatedly had to devote his energies in fighting his opponents because of which he could not become strong in India.

It is said that Babur did not like India. He always longed for his own motherland.

He disliked the Indian climate and its people, but he ruled well.

Even in his short rule he efficiently looked after the state. He made his capital Agra a much better city than what it had been before his rule.

He had the Kabuli Bagh Mosque made for his wife, Mussamat Kabuli Begum.

BABURNAMAH

Babur spoke Turkish and was a follower of Islam. He was a staunch Muslim but was not cruel towards the Hindus. He was also kind to his people in the court.

He was highly educated; a master of Turkish and Persian. He himself wrote the story of his life in Turkish, his mother tongue. It is named 'Baburnamah' or 'Tuzuk-I-Baburi'. It tells us a lot about those times and about Babur.

In his autobiography, he wrote about his personal life as well as the history and geography of the places he lived in.

He loved nature and loved to wander around gardens. He was awed by the flora and fauna of India. He had many gardens made in India.

He was also a great lover of architecture and music.

He has given descriptions of nature and its beauty in this autobiographical work.

The book begins with the fact that Babur became the King of Ferghana, a district of modern Uzbekistan, at the age of twelve.

Babur was a great fighter from the very beginning. He took over the Uzbek city of Samarkand in 1497 and Kabul in 1504.

Babur had to keep fighting to retain this kingdom till he was called to India. He could not stay peacefully in his own kingdom and spent a lot of time away from it.

Babur's daughter, Gulbadan, wrote the biography of Humayun called 'Humayunamah' on Akbar's request. In this biography, she has written a lot about her father Babur and the kind of person he was.

She writes of one incident when Babur sent few gifts from Delhi for his people in Kabul.

There was an old servant in Kabul who was waiting for Babur's gift from the spoils of the Battle of Panipat.

Babur told the messenger to tell the old man that he had sent only one *asharfi*, or gold coin for him. This made the old man sad for three days. Finally when the *asharfi* was to be given to him, he was blind-folded on Babur's instructions.

The gold coin was about 15 kilograms in weight. This heavy coin had a hole in it so that it could be worn around the neck.

When the old man was allowed to open his eyes and see it, he was extremely happy.

He said that he would always keep the gold coin with him and never give it to anyone.

This gold coin was specially minted when Babur started having gold coins made in India.

Babur introduced new things in India. He tried to improve the living condition of the people. His efficiency was not limited only to the battlefield, he even improved the basic infrastructure of the empire.

GIFTS BY BABUR

The coming of Babur changed the history of India. A new way of life started in India.

He gave many gifts to India and brought a lot of beauty with him. He was the first to make gardens in India with waterfalls and canals. This made the grand palaces even more aesthetically appealing.

The Mughals had a grand way of living which can even be seen in their monuments and buildings.

Their affluence was evident everywhere. The royal women and men would wear very rich clothes along with a lot of jewellery. The palaces were richly decorated with the best of silks and velvets. The kings ate in silver and gold utensils.

Babur died after four years. So he could not make the roots of the Mughal Empire very firm.

That is why the Afghan leader, Sher Shah Suri, was able to defeat Babur's son, Humayun.

Humayun lost his Indian territories to Sher Shah Suri as he could not make his empire strong in the beginning.

It was left to Akbar to make India a stronghold of the Mughals.

SACRIFICE

In 1530 A.D., Babur's son Humayun fell sick. When all the doctors gave up, it seemed that Humayun would die. But Babur did not give up. He wanted his son to live a long life.

Babur called many more doctors and did everything he could to get back his son from the jaws of death.

When Babur saw that Humayun was not recovering, he started praying for his health. He asked God to take his life but spare the life of his son.

It seems that God heard his prayers because Babur got the disease that Humayun had.

Babur's daughter, Gulbadan, wrote in her book 'Humayunamah', "On that Tuesday, Babur walked around Humayun in prayer. He raised his head to the saintly 'Karim Illah'. From Wednesday he prayed, 'Oh God, if a life may be taken for a life, I, Babur, give my life and my being for that of my son Humayun.' As he walked around the bed, life drained from him into his son Humayun."

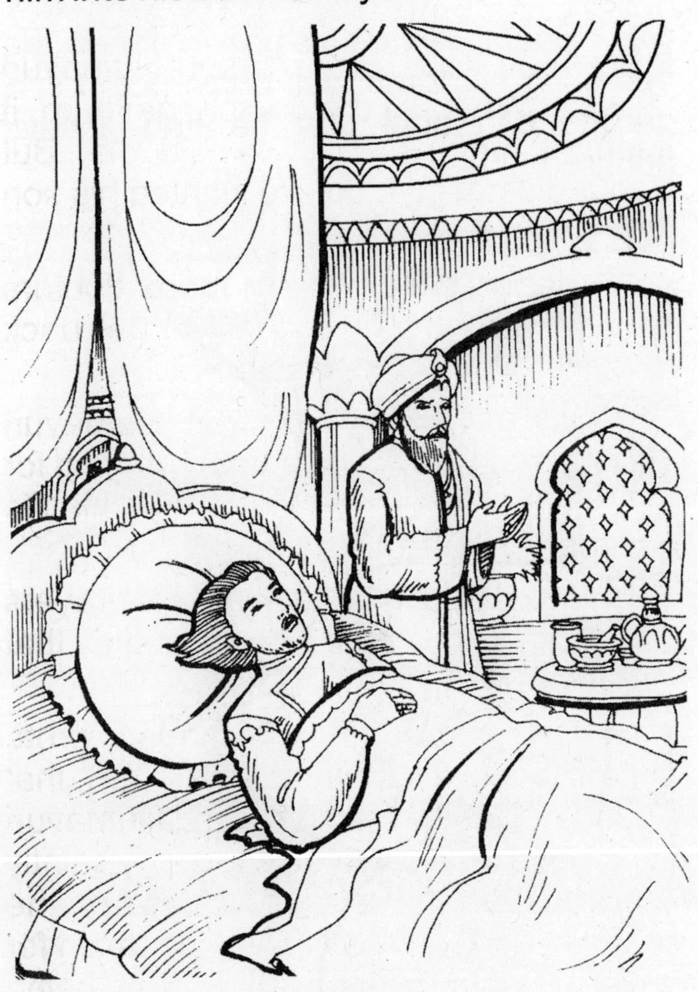

In 1530 A.D., Babur died at the age of 48 years in Agra. Humayun recovered and was made the emperor.

Babur wanted his grave to be in the open. So his tomb was constructed in a garden of Kabul that he had always admired.

THE SCHOLARLY HUMAYUN

In 1530, after Babur's death, Humayun, at the age of twenty-two, became the emperor of the Mughal Empire.

He supported arts and did a lot of painting himself.

He was impressed by the progress of arts in Persia, especially miniature painting.

He introduced the miniature style of Mughal painting in India.

He learnt Turkish, Arabic and Persian. He was good at astrology and mathematics.

Humayun was a good human being and soldier, but he didn't have the qualities of an efficient emperor. He was more of a scholar than a ruler.

He is said to have been absent-minded and indecisive; he found it difficult to decide on a course of action.

Although he fought bravely, he began to be known as a loser because he lost his provinces one by one.

His three brothers Kamran, Askari and Hindal always troubled him. They were mean and nasty, but Humayun was a good man so he always forgave them.

The ten years of Humayun's rule were full of difficulties and troubles.

The Rajputs troubled him, and the Afghans kept fighting with him.

So as an emperor, Humayun had a difficult time in holding on to the reins of his empire.

A THREAD OF BOND

Humayun once received a letter from Queen Karmavati of Chittor.

When Humayun heard of it, he said, "A message from a Rajput Queen to a Mughal Emperor! How strange! Let me know what it says."

Queen Karmavati had sent the letter to tell Humayun that she was facing the danger of an attack from the Gujarat Sultan, Bahadur Shah. He had already killed her husband and was now going to attack her.

She begged Humayun to come and help her like a brother would help a sister.

She sent a *rakhi* (the thread of bond between a brother and a sister in Hindu culture) to Humayun to be tied on his wrist so that he would come and help her.

Humayun said, "She is a Hindu and she has called me, a Muslim, her brother. There will come a day when the Hindus and the Muslims will live as brothers and sisters in India. I am very happy today."

He got his army together and went to help her. But on the way he heard the distressing news of Queen Karmavati's death. She had thrown herself in fire and committed *Jauhar*.

Jauhar refers to the voluntary death committed by the Rajput women to avoid being captured and dishonoured at the hands of their enemies after being defeated by them.

She committed *Jauhar* because the Gujarat Sultan had reached her city. Humayun was too late.

Humayun was very upset that he couldn't save a woman who had considered him her brother.

He vowed that he would kill Bahadur Shah of Gujarat. But this vow couldn't be fulfilled because when Bahadur Shah of Gujarat heard that Humayun and his army were approaching, he ran away.

ON THE RUN

The Afghan chief Sher Shah Suri fought with Humayun and defeated him at the Battle of Chausa in 1539.

In 1540, at the Battle of Kannauj, Humayun was again defeated and had to run away from Delhi and Agra.

Humayun first went to Sind and then fled to Persia (now Iran).

So his first rule over India was from 1530 to 1540.

Humayun was in exile for fifteen years, moving from Sind to Iran and then to Afghanistan. He faced a lot of hardships when he had to run from one place to another.

For sometime he stayed in Sind to protect himself from Sher Shah.

Humayun stayed in the desert for many years till he returned to fight again.

He always thought of taking back his empire from Sher Shah.

In the meantime, Sher Shah had made his kingdom strong. He had become too powerful for Humayun to defeat.

Humayun had to wait till he got help from someone.

During his exile, Humayun fell in love with a thirteen-year-old girl called Hamida Bano. Initially she refused to marry him, but later she gave her consent.

Humayun married her in Sind, and two years later she gave birth to Akbar.

THE GREAT RETURN

In 1546, Sher Shah Suri died in an accidental explosion of gun powder.

Sher Shah Suri's death, along with the fact that the son of Sher Shah was not as strong as his father, strengthened Humayun's hope of regaining his empire.

With the help of the King of Persia, Humayun planned to come and get his throne back.

The King of Persia asked Humayun to convert from Sunni to Shia Islam. Humayun reluctantly converted to Shia Islam. He did this to get substantial support from the King of Persia.

He also took the help of Sultan Tahmasp I. He was able to invade India again with the help of Bairam Khan. He easily captured Punjab.

At that time, the successor of Sher Shah was ruling in Delhi, but he was not strong.

Humayun successfully defeated Ibrahim Suri, the Sultan of Delhi. Then he defeated the King of the Afghans in a battle near Sirhind and became an emperor again.

THE FALL

It was brave and strong of Humayun to be able to get the Mughal Empire back because Sher Shah Suri had made a strong hold over the empire. As the successors of Sher Shah were not very strong, Humayun won.

However, Humayun could not rule for a long time. He ruled only for a year. He reconquered his kingdom in 1555 and died in 1556.

One day, Humayun was watching the planets through his telescope on the terrace of the building 'Din Panah'.

He had always been very fond of astronomy, the study of stars and planets. He had built observatories that lasted for centuries.

While he was busy observing the stars, he heard the call for prayer. He suddenly turned to answer the call for prayer and tripped on his robe and fell down.

He slipped down the steps of the royal library and got injured. The injuries were fatal and lead to his death in 1556.

Before Humayun died, he declared that Akbar would be the next emperor with Bairam Khan as the Regent to help Akbar.

He trusted Bairam Khan as he had helped him regain his kingdom from the successor of Sher Shah Suri.

Sher Shah had done many good things for the people. He had made the Grand Trunk Road and had even made a number of inns for the travellers. He had trees planted on either side of the roads to give shade to the travellers.

Sher Shah had greatly strengthened the government during his reign.

Humayun did not have time to look after the people of India, as he regained his throne in 1555 and died in 1556. He ruled only for a year, and this was the reason why he failed to strengthen the footholds of Mughals in India.

Akbar made up for this and brought big territories under the Mughal Empire.

Humayun's body was buried in the Humayun's tomb, which is an important historical landmark in Delhi.

The making of this tomb was supervised by Humayun's wife, Hamida Begum.

THE YOUNG AKBAR

Akbar was born to Hamida Begum, whom Humayun had married in Sind.

Akbar was born at Umarkot in Sind on 15th October, 1543. This was because his father Humayun had to run away from his kingdom after being defeated by Sher Shah Suri.

He was not born in the comforts of a rich and comfortable palace. And instead of a happy and carefree childhood, he got a tough life of living in the wilderness, travelling from one place to another.

He was not educated as all his time was taken by the travels he had to make with his father.

With Humayun, he moved from Sind to Iran and then to Afghanistan. So he saw more of life and became tough.

When Humayun came back to India and regained his throne, it was then that Akbar saw the refined court culture of Delhi and Agra.

After his father's death in 1556, Akbar was crowned the emperor. He was fourteen years old at that time.

As he was very young, he ruled under the able guidance of Bairam Khan.

In the beginning, Akbar listened to Bairam Khan, but after sometime Akbar wanted to be free of his Regent.

In 1560, Akbar sent Bairam Khan away. On the way to Gujarat, Bairam Khan was murdered.

Akbar was a wise and good king, who efficiently managed his empire. His friendly attitude towards the Hindus was an important factor of his popularity.

He abolished the *jizya tax* which had been exclusively levied on the Hindus. Moreover, he gave important posts to Hindus in his court.

He even married Hindu women. It is said that he had five hundred wives and many of them were Rajput princesses.

Akbar made friends with the Rajputs, but he had to keep fighting with Maharana Pratap.

Maharana Pratap often had to live away from his palace because of his constant wars with Akbar.

Akbar had wanted to marry a princess of Rana's family, but the proposal was rejected.

Akbar then attacked Chittor and killed a number of Rajputs.

Maharana Pratap is said to have taken a vow that he would not sleep on a proper bed till he defeated Akbar.

So he always slept on dry grass spread on the ground. His wife and children also had to face a lot of troubles.

Akbar and Maharana Pratap met in the Battle of Haldighati in 1576.

Maharana Pratap lost the battle and was severely wounded. He slumped on his horse and rode away.

Chetak, his horse, is said to have possessed rare courage and intelligence, along with unwavering faithfulness to his master.

Chetak took him away from the battlefield into the hills, and thus he was saved.

ONE WISH

One thing that troubled Akbar was that he had no son who would inherit his throne after him.

To fulfill his desire for a son, Akbar walked barefoot across a desert to meet Sheikh Salim Chisti, a saint, in Sikri.

The saint lived in a hut on the peak of a hill with thick forests all around. Akbar met the saint. The saint blessed him and said that he would have three sons.

As the saint had prophesied, Akbar had three sons named Salim (who later became Emperor Jahangir), Murad and Daniyal. Murad and Daniyal died while Akbar was still alive.

After Salim's birth, Akbar shifted his capital to the city of Fatehpur Sikri.

He did this because he thought that the city was lucky for him because while he was there he won many wars. There he got a huge gate called 'Bulund Darwaza' made.

'Fateh' means victory. After the winning of various wars, this place was named as Fatehpur Sikri, meaning the place of victory.

There are many beautiful buildings there like the Hawa Mahal and Diwan-e-am.

After the death of Saint Sheikh Salim Chisti in 1572, Akbar got his tomb made in Fatehpur Sikri.

The actual grave has shells covering it, and there is a corridor where people can take a round of the grave.

Initially, the frontage of the tomb was of red sandstone, but later it was covered with marble.

It is said that if women who do not have children tie a thread there, they are blessed by the saint with children.

After bearing their child, they must go and untie the thread from the beautiful marble mesh where they had tied their thread.

Akbar had two lakes made in the city for saving water. But the water available was still not sufficient for everyone.

Akbar played chess in a very interesting way; girls were used as pawns on the huge chessboard made on the ground. Akbar sat on his throne at a height and made the moves.

DIN-I-ILAHI

There is a building in Fatehpur Sikri where Akbar sat on a high throne.

People of different religions assembled below, and Akbar discussed various issues with them.

Akbar was not educated so he could not read, but he had a great love for knowledge. He asked his people to read out books to him. He had built a huge library which had an impressive collection of books. He even got translations from Hindu texts done into the Persian language.

Akbar was also very interested in religion. He believed in Islam, but did not hate the Hindus. He was rather friendly towards them. This was because he was keen to understand different religions.

He used to have people of different religions have discussions on various issues, and then he would listen to them carefully.

He formed a religion called 'Din-i-ilahi'. Din-i-ilahi was a mixture of the good points of different religions. Hindu, Christian and Jesuit priests were consulted, before Akbar decided on the main points of his religion.

He announced the new religion and also told the people that he himself would be the head of 'Din-i-ilahi'.

At that time because of Akbar, most of the people followed it. But this religion gradually lost its popularity after Akbar's death.

Still it speaks a lot for the illiterate Akbar who thought of a new religion based on moral goodness.

It also shows that he wanted to unify all his people with the bond of love and goodness.

While the sultans and emperors who had ruled before him were against the Hindus, Akbar was ready to take the good points of their religion too.

This shows how great Akbar was as an emperor and thinker.

THE NINE GEMS

As a child, Akbar had stayed in Persia when Humayun was exiled from Delhi. This gave him a chance to be acquainted with the Persian style of art and painting.

He cultivated the beauty of Persian architecture by making buildings and monuments in the Persian style.

It is said that he had two hundred painters in his court in Delhi. He also encouraged poets, writers and artists. He admired and respected talented people.

Once Akbar disguised himself and went to hear the holy songs sung by Meera Bai in the temple of Lord Krishna.

Akbar is known for the extra-ordinarily talented people he had in his court.

He had nine extremely talented people in his court, whom he greatly admired.

They were called the Nine Gems or the *Navratans* of Akbar's court, and the emperor was proud of these people.

One of them was Tansen who was blessed with extraordinary singing skills.

It is said that Tansen could make earthen lamps light up while singing the notes of *Raag Deepak*.

Under the open sky, Tansen would sit and sing in the courtyard of the fort. There would be water all around his seat.

Emperor Akbar and the nobles sat in the courtyard around the pool of water. The royal ladies would sit behind a curtain. And everyone would listen to the great Tansen sing.

He would feel very hot after singing the notes of *Raag Deepak*; there was a danger of his getting burnt.

So he would sing the notes of *Raag Megh Malhar*, and it would start raining to cool him.

Birbal, whose name was Mahesh Das, was another gem of his court. Akbar admired Birbal a lot, as he would keep him in a cheerful mood through his wit. Akbar loved to ask riddles and it was only Birbal, with his sharp wit, who could give correct answers.

Akbar sought Birbal's advice on important matters as he was very clever.

There is a grand palace of Birbal in Fatehpur Sikri which reflects the respect he got from Akbar.

Some people say that Akbar even married Birbal's daughter, but it is not a confirmed fact.

There are many anecdotes about how Birbal made Akbar laugh and forget his anger.

Another gem of Akbar's court was Abu Fazl, the writer of 'Akbarnamah'. He also translated the new testament of the Bible into Persian.

His brother Feizi, who was another gem of the court, was a good writer. He translated Sanskrit works into Persian.

Raja Todar Mal, a Rajput, was the wise finance minister of Akbar. He was responsible for keeping the revenue system in order.

Revenue was the method of collecting taxes from the public.

He saw to it that the correct amount of tax was taken. He also made rules to ensure that the collectors did not hurt or trouble the people while collecting taxes. All this greatly helped to improve the finances of Akbar's empire.

Raja Man Singh of Amber was another gem of Akbar's court. He was the grandson of Akbar's father-in-law. Man Singh was an accomplished fighter. He had been the Commander-in-chief of the Mughal army in many battles.

Another gem Abdul Rahim Khan Khanna, the son of Bairam Khan, was a very good poet and had even taught Salim in his childhood.

Faqir Aziao Din and Mullah Do Piazza were the two advisors of Akbar who were also considered as the gems of the royal court.

These great artists, soldiers and writers were well known far and wide.

Akbar was a great emperor under whose patronage art, music and literature flourished.

FAREWELL

Akbar's empire gradually expanded. He ruled over nearly the whole of India and made his empire very strong.

The capital was later shifted to Lahore because Akbar spent a lot of time fighting wars.

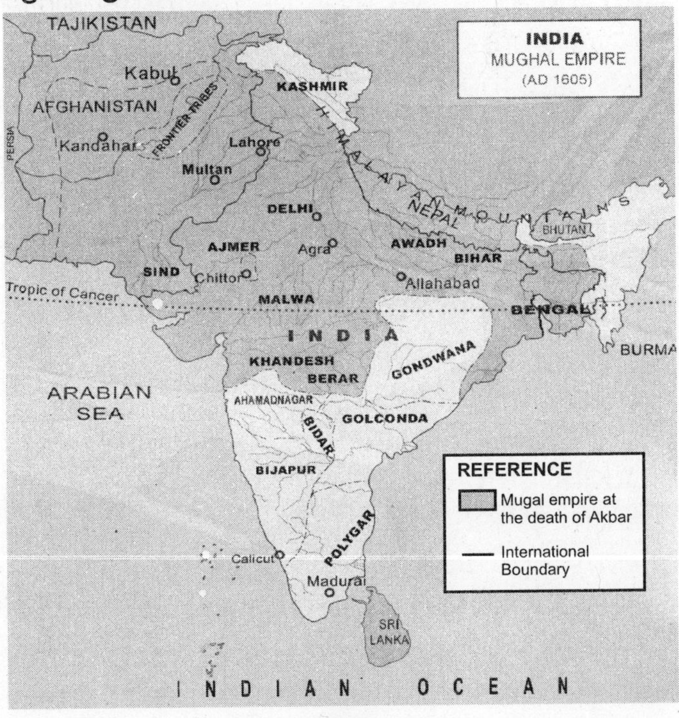

He had inherited a small empire, but he made it big and strong.

On 5th November 1556, he fought the second Battle of Panipat against Hemu (Hemchandra).

Hemu was a military chief of the Afghan king, Muhammad Adil Shah. He had established himself at Chunar.

He wanted to expel the Mughals from India. So he marched with his large army towards Delhi. To counter this, Akbar's army also marched towards Delhi.

The armies met and fought at Panipat. Initially, Hemu with his large army of 1500 war elephants had an edge over Akbar's army.

However, in the middle of the battle a stray arrow struck Hemu in the eye. He fell unconscious on the ground.

When the unconscious Hemu was brought before Bairam Khan and Akbar, Bairam Khan asked Akbar to slay the enemy and earn the Islamic holy title of *Ghazi*.

Akbar then severed the head of the unconscious Hemu. There are certain historians who claim that Akbar just touched the head of Hemu with his sword. He did not kill Hemu himself.

The fall of the leader caused panic in Hemu's army and the wheel of fortune turned. The Mughals won the battle.

Akbar conquered Malwa in 1562, Gujarat in 1572 , Bengal in 1574, Kabul in 1581, Kashmir in 1586 and Kandesh in 1601. He did not directly rule these kingdoms but appointed governors.

Akbar made the Mughal Empire bigger and stronger than Babur had made.

In October 1605 Akbar fell ill and died of slow poisoning. He was buried at Sikandara, near Agra.

His grave was made on the terrace because he wanted his grave to be out in the open. But another grave was made in the hall inside the monument.

SALIM

Jahangir was known as Prince Salim before he was given this title by his father, Akbar.

Akbar called him Shaikhoo. Jahangir was the eldest son.

Salim was born after a lot of prayers. Akbar walked barefoot to meet the great saint Sheikh Salim Chisti for a son.

Jahangir's mother was from a family of Rajputs but her name was not Jhodhabai, as is commonly believed.

The best of education was given to Salim because Akbar himself could not read or write (though he had a great love for learning).

His studies started at the age of 4 years. He was taught Persian, Arabic, Urdu, history, arithmetic, geography and the sciences by teachers as great as Abdul Rahim Khan Khanna, who was a renowned scholar and soldier.

As Salim was allowed to do what he wanted, he became very spoilt and started drinking alcohol at a very young age.

Akbar became worried about his future, so he sent Salim away from the pomp and pageantry of the court.

Salim was given duties to make him a responsible man.

For sometime Salim did give up his bad habits and took part in many armed conquests.

THE PIGEONS

As a child Salim played with Mehr-un-nisa, who later came to be known as Nur Jahan.

As a child, Mehr-un-nisa was a naughty girl. She used to tease Salim a lot.

Akbar was very fond of her and if she did anything naughty, she would hide behind Akbar.

One day Salim asked her to hold two of his precious pigeons while he went for some work.

When he came back, he saw that she had only one pigeon in her hand.

Salim exclaimed, "Just one pigeon! Where is the other pigeon?"

Mehr-un-nisa replied, "It flew away."

Salim angrily said, "What! It flew away! You knew that it was my favourite pigeon. Why didn't you take care of it? How did it fly away?"

Mehr-un-nisa innocently said, “Like this,” and she let the other pigeon fly away too.

When Salim got angry on losing his favourite pigeons, Mehr ran and hid behind Emperor Akbar.

MEHR-UN-NISA

Salim loved Mehr-un-nisa a lot. He wanted to marry her.

Emperor Akbar was also fond of her, but he thought that Salim's marriage to Mehr would be against all forms of propriety as she was a refugee's daughter.

So Akbar ensured that Mehr was married elsewhere while Salim was away from the court on a conquest.

Akbar came to Mehr and said, "I have dreams for Salim. He has to be the Emperor. So it is better that you leave him and marry elsewhere."

Mehr respected Akbar so she promised him that she wouldn't marry Salim.

Mehr-un-nisa, at the age of seventeen, was married to Sher Afghan, who was a governor under the Mughals. He too was a Persian immigrant.

Mehr-un-nisa had a daughter from him called Ladli Begum.

After Akbar's death when Salim was crowned as the emperor, Sher Afghan thought that he and his wife should go and pay their respect to the new emperor. On their way, Sher Afghan was killed but Mehr was safe.

NUR JAHAN

After her husband's death, Mehr came to live in Agra along with her daughter. There she lived as the lady-in-waiting to one of Jahangir's stepmothers called Ruqaiya Sultana Begum.

When Mehr came to the fort of Jahangir, he again expressed his desire to marry her. But keeping her promise to Akbar, Mehr refused his proposal. Jahangir was very upset.

Seeing Jahangir in a bad state and after a lot of persuasion, Mehr agreed to marry him.

It was Jahangir who first gave her the title of Nur Mahal (the light of the palace) and later gave her the title of Nur Jahan (the light of the world). It is said that she was his twentieth wife. She was born in 1577 and lived till the age of sixty-six.

Nur Jahan was a very strong lady. She had a firm hold over Jahangir. He and his ministers sought her advice even in the matters of the state.

She used to sit behind Jahangir even when he sat down in his court to do his work.

She sat behind a *purdah* or curtain, and if she did not agree with what Jahangir was doing, she would place her hand on his back.

After his marriage to Nur Jahan, it is said that Jahangir started having a lot of wine and drugs. So it was Nur Jahan who looked after the empire.

It was she who decided over the promotions and demotions within the royal government.

Furthermore, her power over domestic and foreign trade made her one whose patronage was much sought after.

She even went with him for battles where she would go riding on an elephant.

Once she saved Jahangir by coming back with an army and defeating the enemy.

She personally owned ships that took men and goods to Mecca, a holy city for the believers of Islam.

The extent of her authority can be understood from the fact that coins were minted in her name.

Nur Jahan was also known as an accomplished artist. The designs on her father's tomb of Itmad-ud-daula in Agra are her personal designs.

She drew the designs, and they were copied on the marble of the tomb.

JAHANGIR'S REIGN

Jahangir was thirty-six years old when he started his rule. He ruled from 1605 to 1627.

During his reign, art greatly flourished. Paintings were a source of great aesthetic pleasure for him, and he loved to collect them.

He was a good writer. His love for nature is evident in the description of wildlife in his book 'Tuzk-i-Jahangiri'.

Jahangir was very fond of making monuments. He had many gardens developed in Kashmir.

He did good work in the beginning by setting free the prisoners of war. He maintained the empire as Akbar had left it for him.

His only shortcoming was his love for a life of ease and comfort. Moreover, he would easily believe people and did as they asked him to do.

The persecution and death of Guru Arjun Dev ji, the fifth Sikh guru, happened at the time when Jahangir was the Mughal Emperor. Because of this, the Sikhs turned against the Mughal Emperors.

It was during the rule of Jahangir that the Britisher Sir Thomas Roe came to India.

The Portuguese had already arrived in India. The Britishers were also sent by the Queen of England to start trade with the East.

Sir Thomas Roe came to Jahangir's court to ask for his permission to have exclusive rights to build factories in Surat and other areas.

Had Jahangir refused, the history of India would have taken a different course. But Jahangir gave special permission to the Britishers to trade in India. In return he was given rarities from the European market.

The Britishers who came to India were under the East India Company at that time and not directly under the Queen of England.

Jahangir signed a treaty with the East India Company under which the British merchants were given special rights to trade in India.

THE BELL

Jahangir ordered that a long golden chain with a bell be fixed on the outer wall of his palace. If anybody wanted justice, they could ring the bell at any time.

Once, the bell chain was pulled by a washerwoman.

When Jahangir went outside to listen to the complaint, he saw a washerwoman standing outside and crying.

When he asked her what the matter was, the washerwoman told him that her husband had been killed by an arrow which had the royal sign on it. She had come to ask for justice.

Jahangir saw that the arrow belonged to his wife Nur Jahan. Jahangir loved Nur Jahan a lot. He was highly distressed as according to justice Nur Jahan was to be put to death.

He told the washerwoman that she would get justice the next morning.

Next morning, the anxious courtiers sat down in the court and the washerwoman was called.

Jahangir told her his decision, "This arrow killed your husband. So you kill the husband of the person to whom the arrow belongs."

"What are you saying, My Lord?" said the washerwoman.

Jahangir said, "This arrow which killed your husband belongs to Nur Jahan. So you kill me as I am her husband."

Everyone in the court was very upset on hearing Jahangir's verdict. They started saying that this could not be done.

The washerwoman was also shocked. She could not agree to the verdict that asked for the Emperor's death. So she said, "My Lord, I would never agree to your execution," and she went away.

JAHANGIR'S DEATH

In 1626, while Jahangir and Nur Jahan were coming back from Kashmir, where Jahangir had fallen sick, they were attacked and Jahangir was captured by some rebels. It was Nur Jahan who freed him from the rebels.

Jahangir died on 28th October, 1627 in Lahore. His tomb is in Shahdara. It was constructed on Shah Jahan's order, and it took ten years to complete.

While Jahangir was alive, Nur Jahan had first wanted Khurram (who later came to be known as Shah Jahan) to be the next emperor.

But later when her daughter from her first marriage was married to Khurram's brother, Sharhyar, Nur Jahan wanted Sharhyar to become the king because he was her son-in-law.

She made sure that Jahangir got angry with Khurram and sent him to far off places.

However, after Jahangir's death when Khurram was given the imperial throne, Nur Jahan was imprisoned and exiled to Lahore.

She then lived a lonely life for sixteen years. She died in 1643 and was buried beside Jahangir at Shahdara in Lahore.

KHURRAM

Khurram was born on 15th January, 1592. He was later given the title of Shah Jahan.

His education started when he was four years old. He was exceptionally good at horse riding.

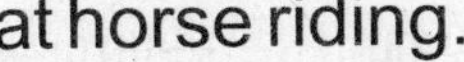

He had three brothers Khusru, Parvez and Shahryar.

But Khurram was the favourite of his grandfather Akbar, who had always thought that he was the cleverest and bravest of all his grandsons.

When Akbar died, Khurram was just thirteen years old. His father Salim then became Emperor Jahangir.

Khurram spent much of his time in looking after the empire. He was sent to places where there were problems because he was considered capable enough to solve them.

Prince Khurram loved Nur Jahan's niece, Anjumand Bano. She was the daughter of Nur Jahan's brother.

Anjumand Bano, born in April 1593, was kind, generous and extremely beautiful. She was a good influence on Shah Jahan.

In 1607, Khurram went to Meena Bazaar, a private market attached to the harem.

Anjumand Bano sat there at a shop with her silks and glass beads.

Khurram saw a piece of glass and asked its price. She said that it was a diamond and he could not afford it.

He took the diamond and gave her ten thousand rupees, which was a lot of money at that time.

Next day, he went to his father and said that he wanted to marry Anjumand, but they got married after five years.

On 10th May, 1612 when Khurram was twenty and Anjumand was nineteen, they got married.

The wedding was a grand one. Jahangir and Shah Jahan went in a procession with nobles, musicians, dancers, acrobats, slaves and priests. Jahangir himself tied a string of pearls around Shah Jahan's neck.

Anjumand Bano (or Mumtaz) and Shah Jahan were married for nineteen years and had fourteen children.

Seven of their children died. The four sons who survived were Dara, Shuja, Aurangzeb and Murad.

The three daughters who survived were Jahan Ara, Roshan Ara and Gauhar Ara.

Mumtaz Mahal always accompanied Shah Jahan wherever he went. Even when she was to give birth to a child, he would take her along when he went for battles.

When Jahangir had passed an order against Shah Jahan, even then they were together. She suffered a lot of misery when Shah Jahan was sick. At that time she asked Shah Jahan to ask his father to pardon him.

WARS

Shah Jahan ruled from 1627 to 1658. But before that he was sent to fight the Rajputs of Mewar under Rana Amar Singh.

So in 1614, Khurram (Shah Jahan was a title that was bestowed on him later) left for Mewar and laid siege to Chittor, but the Rajputs did not give in.

When the siege was taking very long, Khurram took drastic actions. He cut off all supplies of food to the fort of Chittor and even burnt their crops.

The Rajputs were forced to surrender. Khurram returned victorious to Delhi. This made Jahangir very happy with him.

During this time Jahan Ara, the daughter who would look after Shah Jahan in his aging years, was born.

Nur Jahan wanted Khurram to be the next king because then her niece Mumtaz would be the queen and her influence at the court would remain undiminished.

In 1616, Khurram was sent to the Deccan. The Deccan rulers felt threatened by the strong Mughal army so they asked for peace.

Khurram even defeated the Rajput King of Baglana and Bundelkhand.

He also fought against the King of Bijapur and Golconda.

There was a battle waged to send back the Portuguese who were in Bengal.

When Khurram came back with his army from the Deccan, he was asked to go and tackle Malik Ambar. He accepted the task.

He knew that this mission to the Deccan would not be easy because Malik Ambar was quite strong.

Khurram was greatly inspired by 'Baburnamah', the book on Babur. So like Babur, he said, "I will not drink wine till Malik Ambar is defeated."

All the wine was drained away, and the gold and silver wine glasses were broken and given to the poor.

Then Khurram and his army marched to the Deccan. On reaching his destination, he was informed that the Mughals were losing.

Everyone told him to wait till the rains were over. But he made his army attack them then and there.

The enemy was shocked by this sudden attack, and it was this unexpected attack that made the Mughals victorious in this battle.

Khurram came back feeling great, but now Nur Jahan's attitude towards him had changed.

Her daughter by her first marriage to Sher Afghan was married to Khurram's youngest brother, Shahryar.

Now Nur Jahan thought about her daughter first and not her niece. She wanted her own daughter to be the queen.

Her attitude towards Khurram changed as now she did not want him to be the emperor.

She made sure that Jahangir kept Khurram away from Delhi, as she now wanted Shahryar to be the king.

REBELLION

Jahangir again sent Shah Jahan to the Deccan. From the Deccan, he wanted Shah Jahan to go to Kandahar.

Shah Jahan understood that Nur Jahan was trying to keep him away from Delhi.

So Shah Jahan told his father that he would go to Kandahar only if he was given more powers.

Nur Jahan then instigated Jahangir against Shah Jahan. All his money was taken away on the order of his father, Emperor Jahangir.

Then Shah Jahan fought with his father, in a region near Delhi, but was defeated.

For three years, Shah Jahan had to run from one place to another with his family.

When Shah Jahan became sick, Mumtaz told him to ask his father for forgiveness.

Jahangir said that he would have to give some land back and send his sons, Dara and Aurangzeb, as hostages.

After one and a half years, Shah Jahan came to know that Jahangir was sick in Kashmir.

Then on his way to Delhi, Jahangir was caught by rebels and later he died.

Shah Jahan's brothers Khusrau and Parvez had already died, and now he had to fight with Shahryar to become the emperor.

After Jahangir's death, Shahryar had declared at Lahore that he would be the emperor.

Mumtaz Mahal's father, Asaf Khan, fought with Shahryar and sent a messenger to Shah Jahan, telling him to come to Agra at once.

Asaf Khan defeated Shahryar, and Shah Jahan was crowned as the emperor on 24th February, 1628 at Agra.

Dara and Aurangzeb were also freed by Asaf Khan, and the family was reunited.

Mumtaz had fourteen children, and the day after the birth of her fourteenth baby, Gauhar Ara, she died.

At that time, she was with Shah Jahan at a battle. Before dying, she took three promises from Shah Jahan.

Mumtaz asked Shah Jahan to make a tomb for her that would make people remember their love.

She asked him not to remarry and to treat his children well.

Shah Jahan promised her to fulfill all the three wishes.

Her death completely shattered him; his hair turned grey and he seemed to age overnight.

For two years he did not allow any celebrations in the palace.

THE TAJ MAHAL

The beautiful Taj Mahal, the epitome of beauty and love, was built by Shah Jahan in memory of his beloved wife, Mumtaz Mahal.

Twenty thousand people worked for seventeen years to make this marble monument. Thirty-seven creative experts came from all over the world.

There are different opinions regarding the monument's cost. Some estimate its cost to be 40 million rupees, and others estimate the cost to be 90 million rupees.

The Taj Mahal, the wonder in marble, is a blend of Indian, Persian, Islamic and Turkish architecture.

There are many Hindu influences on the building of the monument too.

The dome is an upside down lotus resting on its petals, and on the ceiling is the drawing of the sun.

The Hindu influence on the Taj Mahal comes as no surprise as Shah Jahan's mother was a Hindu, the daughter of Udai Singh of Marwara in Rajasthan.

The four minarets of the Taj Mahal are built in such a manner that if they fall, they will fall away from the main building.

The whole monument is made of marble. Semi-precious stones were brought from far away lands for the Taj.

The design and the manner in which the main building is set against the River Yamuna makes it an immensely attractive sight.

The Taj Mahal looks wonderful in the moonlight. Its beauty keeps changing with the changing light of the sun and the moon.

The calligrapher of the Taj was Amanat Khan Shirazi. His name appears at the end of an inscription on one of the gates of the Taj.

It is said that when the person who made the Taj Mahal was told by Shah Jahan that his arms would be cut so that he won't be able to make another such monument, he took Shah Jahan's permission to go up the Taj Mahal once. He hit his hammer somewhere on the top, through which it is said that the first drop of monsoon falls on the grave of Shah Jahan.

Later Aurangzeb took Shah Jahan as a prisoner and kept him in that part of the Red Fort from where he could see the Taj Mahal. It was his daughter Jahan Ara who looked after Shah Jahan.

When Shah Jahan's eyes became very weak, as he grew old, he could see the Taj Mahal reflected in a small glass fixed in the wall of the fort.

It is said that Shah Jahan wanted to make another Taj in black marble, on the opposite side of the Taj Mahal, to enshrine his own remains. He even started building it. But Aurangzeb stopped it because by then he had made Shah Jahan a captive.

Shah Jahan was buried in the Taj near the grave of his wife Mumtaz Mahal when he died in 1666 at the age of seventy-four.

The real graves of Mumtaz Mahal and Shah Jahan are in the basement, but another pair of graves are made in the room above.

Shah Jahan is known for the wonderful buildings and grand monuments he got made.

Shah Jahan moved his capital from Agra to Delhi, and this paved the way for many beautiful and great buildings in Delhi like the Red Fort and the Jama Masjid.

In Lahore, the Shalimar Gardens, the Moti Masjid (also called the Pearl Mosque) and sections of the Lahore Fort were constructed by Shah Jahan.

This lover of architectural beauty gave grand monuments to the succeeding generations.

However, he spent so much on these monuments that he almost exhausted the royal coffers. This was one of the reasons of the slow decline of the Mughal Empire.

The Taj Mahal was his greatest gift. It is considered as one of the modern wonders of the world.

EARLY DAYS

Aurangzeb was a staunch believer of Islam.

He spent his childhood and teenage as a hostage with his brother Dara at his grandfather Jahangir's palace.

When Jahangir died in 1627 and Shah Jahan became the emperor, he went back to his parents.

He was made the Governor of the Deccan, but at that time there was peace there.

He fought with his brothers to become the emperor. He used cunning strategies such as taking the side of one and later going against him.

He was not the eldest but was able to defeat his elder brothers, Dara Shukoh and Shuja, and his younger brother Murad to become the emperor.

Aurangzeb was cruel not only towards his brothers but also towards his father. After he took over the imperial throne, he took his father Shah Jahan as a prisoner.

SIMPLE LIVING

Few people know that Aurangzeb led a plain and simple life, without the luxuries enjoyed by the Mughal Emperors before him.

He believed in Islam to the extent that he hated the Hindus. His intolerant attitude towards other religions is evident from the fact that he imposed tax on non-believers, destroyed temples of the Hindus and forced people to convert to Islam.

He was a religious man who said his prayers even in the middle of a battle.

He did not allow music, painting or any of the fine arts in the court. He enforced laws against drinking and gambling.

He never took money for himself from the treasury. This was really remarkable because the other emperors had led very rich lifestyles.

He copied the Islamic holy book 'Quran' himself and sold these works to earn his living.

Aurangzeb was so careful not to spend the money of the empire that every day he would knit a haj cap. He earned his living by selling these caps.

AT WAR

Aurangzeb is infamous for his cruel attitude towards the Hindus.

He spoilt various temples of the Hindus including Krishna's birth temple in Mathura, the Kashi Vishwanath temple, the Vishnu temple, etc.

He destroyed many other Hindu temples and built mosques in their places.

He closed down non-Muslim schools. The Muslim schools called *madarsas* were not closed down.

He abolished *Sati,* the practice of a Hindu wife killing herself in the funeral pyre of her husband.

The Hindus, who were accustomed to live according to the Hindu laws, found themselves at odds when faced with the Islamic laws that were forced on them by Aurangzeb.

He also forced many Hindus to change their religion and convert to Islam.

The Hindus surely didn't approve of this.

Throughout his reign, Aurangzeb was engaged in wars. He was against the Hindus, but in his huge army he had many Rajput soldiers. He favoured Rajputs in his army, as they were brave and sincere fighters.

His rule is marked with regular wars with the Marathas and the Sikhs.

He fought many wars with the kings of Punjab, Bijapur and Golconda.

In the last twenty years of his life, he kept fighting in the Deccan.

He fought with the brave Sikhs in 1670. Guru Tegh Bahadur ji, the ninth Sikh guru, was arrested and beheaded when Aurangzeb failed to convert him to Islam. The Sikhs were outraged at this barbarous act of Aurangzeb.

The Sikhs were not an army in the beginning when Guru Nanak dev ji started this religion. However, to fight against the tyranny of the Mughals such as Jahangir and Aurangzeb, they made a forceful army.

Guru Gobind Singh ji became the tenth Sikh guru. He started an army with each member called a *Khalsa*, meaning saint-soldier.

SHIVAJI

From 1657 till the end of his rule, Aurangzeb had to constantly fight with Shivaji.

Shivaji troubled him by fighting in a style known as Guerilla warfare.

Shivaji would hide with his army and then suddenly attack the Mughal army.

The Mughals would be surprised, as they would be attacked when they least expected it.

Shivaji was a wily leader. An evidence of his cleverness was the way he dealt with Afzal Khan of Bijapur.

When Afzal Khan could not defeat Shivaji, he asked Shivaji to meet him saying that he wanted to talk about peace and friendship.

When they met in the open, both had armed themselves.

The tall and strong Afzal Khan tried to embrace Shivaji to kill him, but Shivaji had worn his famous tiger claws. They were four curved claws worn on the hand.

Shivaji clawed Afzal Khan and killed him.

So Aurangzeb was very careful while dealing with Shivaji. He sent the brother of Mumtaz Mahal, who was one of the few men he trusted, to deal with Shivaji. His name was Shaista Khan.

Shaista Khan was a good general and was loyal to Aurangzeb. He was successful in defeating Shivaji.

Once Shaista Khan was staying in the well guarded Lal Mahal of Pune. The Marathas were not allowed in the city.

A marriage party had got special permission to take out a wedding procession. Shivaji and his men entered the city of Pune, disguised as members of the wedding procession.

They secretly entered the house where Shaista Khan was staying.

They broke a wall and attacked Shaista Khan and his men. They killed his son but couldn't kill him. They even killed a man mistaking him for Shaista Khan.

When they attacked, Shaista Khan jumped out of the window. As he was jumping out of the window, they saw him and threw a dagger at him.

His thumb got cut, but he escaped. He was taken away safely by his servants. The Marathas went away without being caught by anyone.

Shivaji was at constant war with Aurangzeb. To keep the Marathas under check, Aurangzeb had to shift to the Deccan. He moved his court to Aurangabad and kept fighting with him.

SHIVAJI'S ESCAPE

Shivaji gained kingship in 1674 and ruled till 1680. He was called *Chhattrapati Shivaji*.

Shivaji once sent a letter to Aurangzeb saying that he wanted to meet him to offer him his friendship, but he had actually planned to kill Aurangzeb.

Shivaji was called to the court in Agra, but when he went there, he was insulted.

He was made to sit with the common people and not with the nobles in the court. This was done not only because Aurangzeb wanted to insult him, but also because he did not want Shivaji to come near him.

Feeling insulted, Shivaji got angry and tried to walk away from the court, but Aurangzeb had him arrested. He was kept under house arrest along with his son Sambhaji.

Slowly the news spread that Shivaji was sick and was soon going to die.

He told Aurangzeb that he would like to make up for the sins he had committed.

He asked for Aurangzeb's permission to send sweets and other gifts for the poor. As Aurangzeb was a very religious man, he agreed to this at once.

Every day, each and every basket was checked by Polad Khan before sending them out. But he found only sweets in them.

Slowly the guards became careless and did not check the baskets thoroughly.

Then one day, Shivaji put his son in one basket and in another he sat himself.

That day too Polad Khan checked some baskets and found only sweets in them.

He did not check the baskets in which Shivaji and his son were sitting.

After the baskets were taken out, Polad Khan went to see Shivaji in his room to make sure he was there.

He saw a man lying down covered with a blanket with his hand outside the blanket. On one of the fingers was the royal ring of Shivaji.

In this way Shivaji escaped from the Mughal prison. He was healthy and not sick. All this sickness was his plan to escape from the prison because Aurangzeb wanted to hang him.

Polad Khan was thus satisfied that Shivaji was inside his own room.

The man who was lying in the place of Shivaji was Hiroji. He was wearing the ring given by Shivaji. A young boy was sitting near him.

The date on which Shivaji was to be hanged was drawing closer and Aurangzeb was eagerly waiting for it.

A day before the day of hanging, Hiroji got up and wore his own clothes. He went to the guards and said that he had to go and get some medicines as Shivaji was felling very sick.

He went out with the other boy and never came back to the prison again.

Next day, when Polad Khan came to take Shivaji for his execution, he saw Shivaji lying without making any movement.

He thought that Shivaji was already dead. But when he removed the blanket, there was nobody there.

Polad Khan was dumbstruck, and Aurangzeb was furious when he came to know that Shivaji had escaped.

By that time Shivaji, along with his son Sambhaji, was on his way towards his kingdom.

Aurangzeb was troubled by the Marathas even after that but he did not give up.

He stayed in Aurangabad to fight with the Marathas.

Aurangzeb died in the year 1707. His reign lasted for forty-nine years.

During his long reign, he greatly extended the frontiers of the Mughal Empire but was not able to maintain it. The vastness of the empire made its army and bureaucracy weak, and this made it an easy target of invasion.

Moreover, Aurangzeb did not have trustworthy men whom he could send to take care of the far flung regions of his empire.

He had to stay away from his palace and court in Agra for a long time.

He was buried according to his will in an open air grave with no tomb on top.

His simple, open-air grave is a nearly square platform in Kuldabad near Aurangabad.

THE MUGHAL EMPIRE

The Mughals came from the famous Timurid dynasty. Babur was related to Timurlane from his mother's side.

He was also related to the great fighter Chengis Khan.

The Mughal dynasty came to India when Babur came to India in 1526.

Their main and strong kings ruled till 1707 when Aurangzeb died.

The Mughal Empire comprised of North India under Babur's rule. Akbar had greatly expanded the Mughal Empire.

Jahangir and Shah Jahan had maintained the empire, and Aurangzeb had greatly extended the frontiers of the empire.

After a long time, nearly all the states of India were again under one consolidated rule.

The Mughal Empire seemed big and strong, and its glory and fame spread far and wide.

But gradually the empire became weak, though it seemed to be big and strong.

There were many reasons for the decline of the Mughal Empire. One of it was the harsh treatment that the Hindus (who formed the majority) received at the hands of Aurangzeb.

Akbar had used up a lot of money in building Fatehpur Sikri and other monuments.

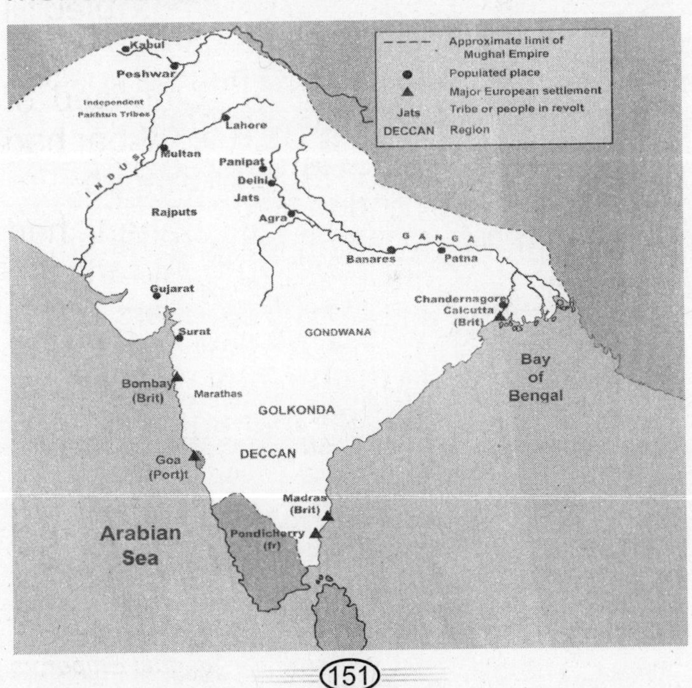

Jahangir had spent a lot of money on his rich lifestyle, drinks and drugs to which he was addicted.

Shah Jahan had spent a massive amount of money on the Taj Mahal and the other monuments he had built.

The Taj Mahal proved very costly, and its maintenance was done by the money that came from the revenue from villages.

Aurangzeb had spent a lot of money on wars, especially with the Marathas.

All this left very little money in the empire's treasury. A weak financial position was a major reason of its downfall.

Moreover, Aurangzeb's harsh treatment of the Hindus made the Mughals unpopular. Many Hindu kings were angry with him.

The kings who came after Aurangzeb were not capable rulers, they were rather weak. They could not manage the huge empire.

After Aurangzeb's death when the throne passed on to his son, he was so old that he could only live for a few more years before passing on the throne again.

There were many kings who wanted to be free. Soon after 1707, these kings declared that they were not under the Mughal rule any more.

The later Mughal Emperors were not strong enough to defeat these rebels.

After the death of Aurangzeb, the Mughals gradually became less important.

With the British gaining importance, the Mughal Empire became all the more weak.

Moreover, there was also a lot of uncertainty about who would be the next emperor. No one in the royal family was safe because people were jealous of each other.

Whenever a king died, there would be plots to kill members of the royal family and wars for deciding which son would be the next king.

In a single year, there were two emperors who were crowned and then dethroned.

Though the Mughal dynasty prevailed till 1857, the Mughals after Aurangzeb were weak rulers.

By 1857 many Mughal Emperors had come and gone without regaining their former glory. They kept fighting either amongst themselves or with other invaders.

Bahadur Shah Zafar was the last Mughal Emperor of India. He planned to fight against the British in the first war of India's independence in 1857.

With the Rani of Jhansi, Nana Rao, Tantia Tope, he also fought against the British.

But the British forces defeated the Indian forces, and nearly all the leaders died.

The last Mughal Emperor, Bahadur Shah Zafar, was sent to Burma (now Myanmar) by the British.

He constantly asked the British to let him come back to Delhi if only to die, but they refused.

Bahadur Shah Zafar died in Rangoon (in Burma) and was buried there.

The last Mughal Emperor was just allowed to stay in the Red Fort of Delhi. He had no freedom, and he could only do what the British asked him to do.

That was the sad end of the grand Mughal dynasty which had reigned for a long time in India.

WHAT A LIFE!

The Mughals had earned a lot of wealth and their way of life was full of pomp and glory.

The forts were well built, and the palaces were very richly decorated.

The gardens had water canals, fountains, sprinklers, waterfalls and greenery which added to the beauty of the palaces.

These were good ways of keeping cool in the heat of India because when the breeze blew, the water would make the warm air cool.

The open and airy Hawa Mahal in Fatehpur Sikri shows how in the intense heat too the Mughal Emperors could keep themselves cool.

Akbar slept on a bed under which there was water. In this way he kept himself cool in the hot weather of India.

Various talented and renowned musicians, singers and painters gave aesthetic pleasure to the Mughal Emperors.

They certainly lead a luxurious life, but they also had to face a lot of problems. They had to go out for months fighting their battles in hot, rainy or cold weather.

During wars, they would have to stay away from their wives and children.

If they took their family along, then the family had to suffer the hardships with the emperor.

Moreover, the kings were never at peace because they always had the fear that someone might try and kill them to become the emperor.

There were a lot of intrigues and plans being made against the emperor in the family as well as amongst the generals.

Even brothers were not to be trusted because anyone could kill anyone.

After Jahangir's and Shah Jahan's death, a lot of wars of succession were fought amongst brothers.

Though Aurangzeb won, it is said that Dara Shukoh was a liberal minded man. He could have been another Akbar in his friendship with the Hindus.

People say that if Dara had been the king, the position of the Mughals might have strengthened. In that case the later Mughals would not have lost their significance.

Aurangzeb wasted a lot of money and time in fighting against the Hindus. In a way, he started the downfall of the Mughal Empire.

In India, the main Mughals were the first six but the Mughal dynasty ruled from 1526 to1857.

MUGHAL EMPERORS FROM 1526 A.D. TO 1857A.D.

1526-1530	BABUR
1530-1556	HUMAYUN
1556-1605	AKBAR
1605-1628	JAHANGIR
1628-1659	SHAH JAHAN
1659- 1707	AURANGZEB
1707-1712	SHAH ALAM I
1712-1713	JAHANDAR SHAH
1713-1719	FURRUKHSIYAR
1719	SHAH JAHAN II
1719	RAFI UD DAULAT
1719	NIKUSIYAR
1720	MOHAMMAD IBRAHIM
1720-1748	MOHAMMAD SHAH
1748-1754	AHMAD SHAH
1754-1759	ALAMGIR II
1759-1760	SHAH JAHAN III
1760-1806	SHAH ALAM II
1806-1837	AKBAR SHAH II
1837-1857	BAHADUR SHAH ZAFAR